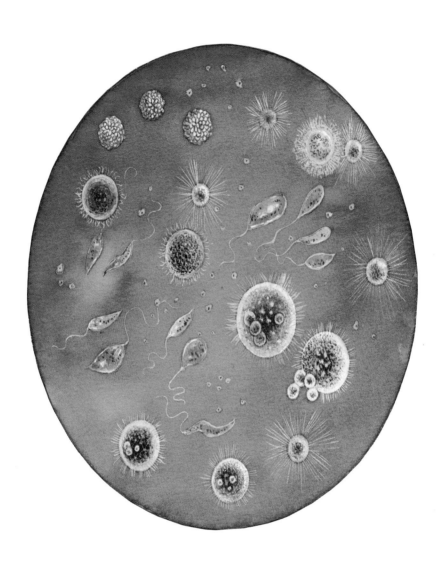

The Four Elements

WATER

Connor Dayton

Illustrations by Cecco Mariniello

WINDMILL
BOOKS ™

New York

Published in 2015 by Windmill Books, An Imprint of Rosen Publishing
29 East 21st Street, New York, NY 10010

Illustrations by Cecco Mariniello
Computer graphics by Roberto Simoni

Photo Credits: p. 9 Dieter Hawlan/iStock/Thinkstock; p. 11 Khoroshunova Olga/Shutterstock.com; p. 16 Stephane Bidouze/Shutterstock.com; p. 20 (left) Carina-Foto/Shutterstock.com; p. 20 (right) Jean Michel Georges/iStock/Thinkstock; pp. 22-23 VLADJ55/Shutterstock.com; p. 25 Alexey Kamenskiy/Shutterstock.com.

Library of Congress Cataloging-in-Publication Data

Dayton, Connor.
Water / by Connor Dayton.
     pages cm. — (The four elements)
Includes index.
ISBN 978-1-4777-9267-4 (library binding) — ISBN 978-1-4777-9268-1 (pbk.) — ISBN 978-1-4777-9265-0 (6-pack)
1. Water—Juvenile literature. 2. Four elements (Philosophy)—Juvenile literature.
I. Title.
GB662.3.D398 2015
553.7—dc23
                                    2013050483

Manufactured in the United States of America

CPSIA Compliance Information: Batch # BW14WM: For Further Information contact Windmill Books, New York, New York at 1-866-478-0556
Windmill Books wishes to thank AD Books for original creation of content in this book.

Contents

The Four Elements

Ancient peoples thought the world was made of four **elements**. These elements were water, fire, air, and earth. We now know that the Earth is made of many more elements. We still use the term element for these materials. There are 92 elements on Earth, while even more exist in space.

This series looks at the science behind the original elements. Even though none of them is what we now know to be an element, each is very important. Without water, life could not exist!

Water: A True Friend

Water is a part of our lives. From swimming to bathing to washing our clothes, we depend on this **liquid** in many different ways.

We cannot live without water, because our bodies need it to work.
In fact, humans can only survive for a few days without drinking water.

Water, Water Everywhere

What do you see when you picture water? Maybe you see a glass of drinking water, or a lake or river. Water is also in places where you can't see it. Plants, trees, and clouds are all partly made of water.

Even your body is more than half water. This doesn't mean that there are rivers and lakes under your skin. But every part of your body is partly made of water.

You may have heard someone call water "H_2O." This is because water is made of two elements, called hydrogen (H) and oxygen (O). Water is two parts hydrogen and one part oxygen. This is why it is called H_2O.

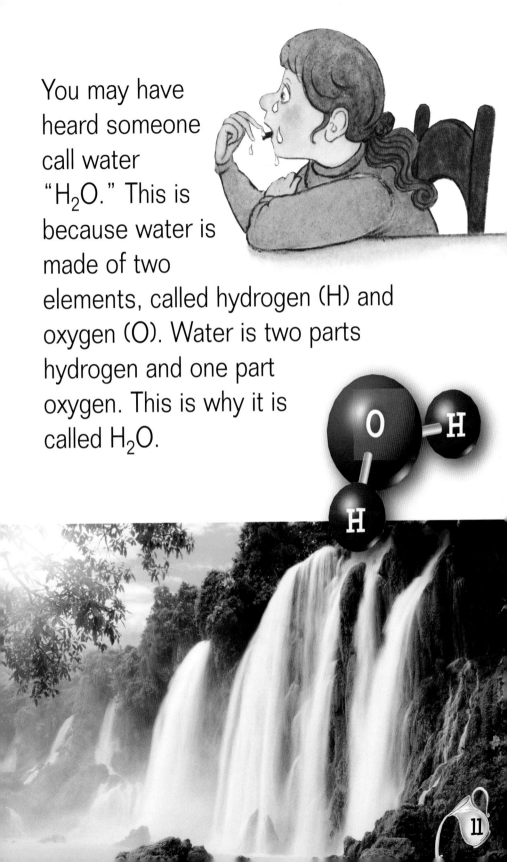

A Bucket Filled with Life

The first life on Earth began in water. They were simple creatures, but every type of animal and plant on Earth today is related to the first life forms.

Simple life forms, like **plankton**, are still all over the ocean. If you took a small bucket to the ocean and filled it with water, you would have hundreds of thousands of tiny, tiny plankton in your bucket!

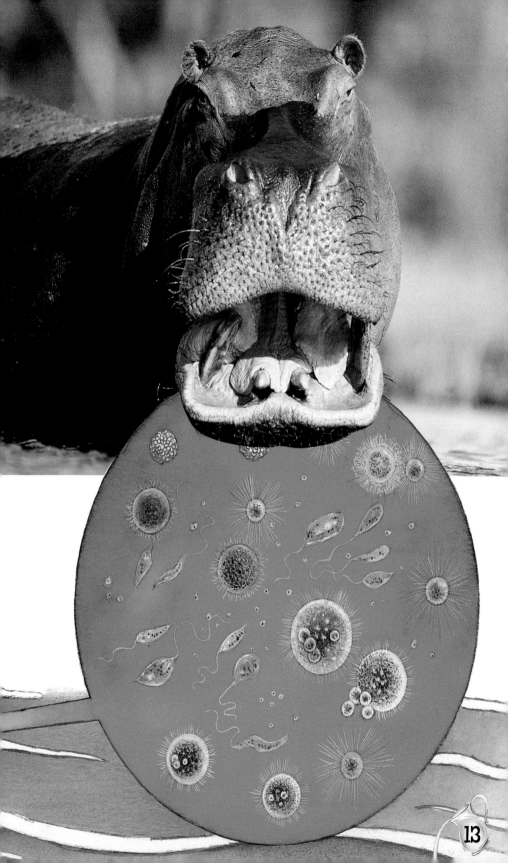

13

States of Water

Water on Earth exists in three forms. The **solid** form of water is ice. Ice is not just something you use to cool down a drink. Ice is found naturally on Earth in **glaciers** and at the North and South Poles. If ice is taken out of a cold place, it will melt and become a liquid. Liquid water fills all the oceans, lakes, and rivers of planet Earth.

When water boils, some of the water becomes a **gas**, water **vapor**. If that water vapor cools, it will condense, or turn from a gas back into a liquid.

Solids, liquids, and gases are called the states of matter. All elements can be in these states, even metals.

The Water Cycle

The **water cycle** describes how water naturally moves around Earth's environment. Water on the Earth's surface **evaporates**, or changes from a liquid to a gas, and rises into the air. This gas is called vapor.

Vapor collects in the air to form clouds. When these clouds get colder, the vapor falls back to Earth as liquid water. But most of us call it rain!

When falling rain
cools more quickly,
it becomes snow or
hail. Hail is ice that
falls from clouds.

The Thirsty Earth

Plants need water to grow. It may look like plants take in water from their leaves after a rainstorm. Actually, plants have **roots** deep in the ground, which take in water from the soil.

Much of our food comes from plants. Over thousands of years, farmers have

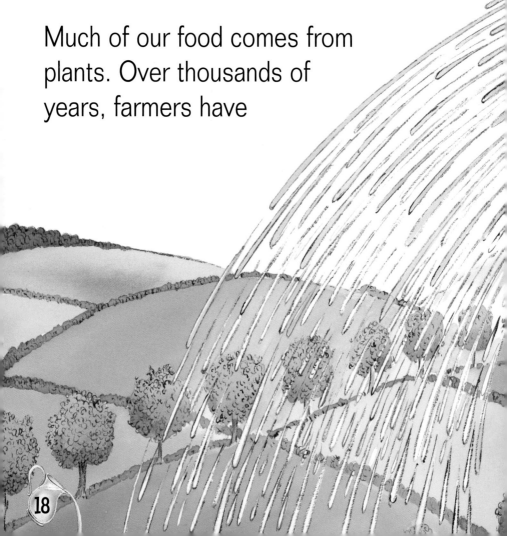

learned how to bring water to their plants through ditches or pipes. This is called **irrigation**.

Salty Water

Most of the world's water is in oceans. Ocean water is too salty to drink. Still, the ocean is very important to people. All our seafood comes from oceans. Also, we use boats that travel around the world's oceans to move things from country to country.

Water Is an Artist

Water has the power to shape the land. Water flows down mountains and forms rivers. Rivers flow over the same land for millions of years and cut into it. This is how the Grand Canyon was formed!

Water also breaks down solid rock. Sand is formed when ocean water washes over rocks for many years. Water that drips through caves can break down the rock into tiny bits. It can then redeposit them, creating beautiful structures called stalactites and stalagmites.

Putting Water to Work

Have you ever seen a mill? A mill uses the power of water to turn a wheel. The wheel then powers a machine inside the mill. This machine might might make flour, paper, lumber, or many other things.

Dams hold back rivers. A dam may let a small amount of water through, though. This flow of water can power a machine that creates electricity. The electricity can then be used in people's homes!

Wild Water

Water is necessary for life. Still, water can be harmful to us. If it rains too much, floods can happen. Floods often ruin houses. They can also destroy a farmer's field.

Having no rain or water over a long period of time can also be dangerous. This is called a **drought**. Droughts make farming very difficult.

Dirty Water, Clean Water

When we use water, it does not just go down the drain and disappear. Dirty water goes back into rivers, lakes, and oceans. Sometimes people or factories may dump trash or waste into clean water. **Pollution** happens when we make water dirty.

But there is good news. Many people are working to keep the world's water clean and safe. Does your town have safe drinking water? Is there a polluted river in your area? Get your community together to make sure that this important element is safe and available to all.

Glossary

drought (DROWT) A period of dryness that causes harm to crops.

elements (EH-luh-ments) The basic things of which all other things are made.

evaporates (ih-VA-puh-rayts) Changes from a liquid to a gas.

gas (GAS) A fluid, like water or air, with no solid shape.

glaciers (GLAY-shurz) Large masses of ice that move down mountains or along valleys.

irrigation (ih-rih-GAY-shun) The carrying of water to land through ditches or pipes.

liquid (LIH-kwed) Matter that can be poured.

plankton (PLANK-ten) Plants and animals that drift with water currents.

pollution (puh-LOO-shun) Man-made wastes that harm Earth's air, land, or water.

roots (ROOTS) The parts of plants or trees that are underground.

solid (SOH-led) Matter that is hard.

vapor (VAY-per) A liquid that has turned into a gas.

water cycle (WAH-ter SY-kul) The natural process of water drying up and forming clouds then falling back to Earth as rain.

Further Reading

Gosman, Gillian. *What Do You Know About the Water Cycle?*
New York: PowerKids Press, 2014.

McAllan, Kate. *Water Is Precious*. New York: PowerKids
Press, 2013.

Owen, Ruth. *Energy from Oceans and Moving Water*. New
York: PowerKids Press, 2013.

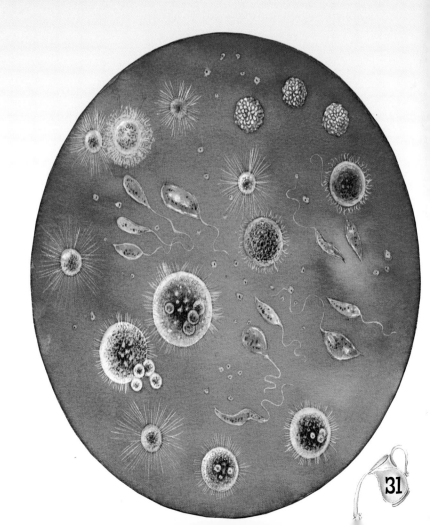

Index

Websites

For web resources related to the subject of this book, go to:
www.windmillbooks.com/weblinks and select this book's title.